For my two little bugs

A Ant

Did you know ants are super strong?

They can carry things much heavier than themselves, like food or even other ants! Ants also talk to each other by leaving scented trails. And did you know ants live in big families called colonies?

Each ant has a special job, like finding food, taking care of babies, or protecting the nest. Ants work together as a team to make sure their colony stays safe and well-fed.

Length: 0.27 in

B Bee

Did you know bees are super busy?

They visit lots of flowers every day to collect nectar and pollen. This helps them make honey and also helps plants grow new seeds and fruits!

Bees have a special dance called the "waggle dance" to tell their friends where the best flowers are.

Bees live together in big groups called colonies, and each bee has an important job to help the colony survive.

Length: 0.55 in

 Cicada

Did you know they can stay underground for a really long time?

Some cicadas live underground as nymphs for 13 or even 17 years before they come out as adults!

When they finally emerge, male cicadas make a loud buzzing sound to attract mates.

They have special organs called "tymbals" that vibrate rapidly to create this noise.
Cicadas often come out in huge groups called "broods", where millions of them appear together.

Length: 1.5 in

D Dragonfly

Did you know they are amazing flyers?

They can hover in the air, fly backwards, and even change direction instantly! Dragonflies have big eyes that help them see all around, including spotting prey like mosquitoes.

They're also ancient insects that have been around for over 300 million years! Dragonflies start their lives underwater as nymphs, hunting small insects and growing until they're ready to become flying adults.

Length: 4 in

Earwig

Did you know earwigs have pincers?

They use these pincers at the end of their abdomen called "cerci" to defend themselves and catch prey like small insects. Despite their name, earwigs don't crawl into people's ears!

They prefer dark, damp places like under rocks or in garden soil. Earwigs are also good mothers. They protect their eggs and take care of their young until they can fend for themselves.

Length: 0.8 in

F Firefly

Did you know fireflies light up to communicate?

They produce a glowing light in their abdomen using a chemical reaction called bioluminescence. Each species of firefly has its own unique pattern of flashing lights to attract mates.

Fireflies are also known as lightning bugs because of their ability to produce flashes of light. They're most active at night, flying around and flashing their lights to find each other.

Length: 1 in

Grasshopper

Did you know they can jump really far?

They have powerful hind legs that allow them to leap great distances, sometimes up to 20 times their body length!

Grasshoppers make music too. They rub their legs against their wings to create a chirping sound, which they use to communicate with other grasshoppers. These insects also have big eyes and can see all around them, helping them spot predators like birds and lizards.

Length: 2.75 in

Hornet

Did you know they are big and powerful flyers?

They can zoom through the air at high speeds, making them impressive hunters. Hornets also live in large nests with thousands of other hornets. They work together to build their nests out of paper-like material made from chewed wood fibers mixed with their saliva.

Hornets are protective of their nests and can sting multiple times if they feel threatened. Despite their stings, hornets play an important role in ecosystems by hunting other insects and helping control their populations.

Length: 2.2 in

Inchworm

Did you know they move in a unique way?

Also known as measuring worms. They are fascinating caterpillars! They loop their bodies forward, stretching out like a measuring tape, and then scrunching up to move forward again.

Inchworms are great at camouflaging. They often look like twigs or leaves, which helps them hide from predators like birds. These caterpillars will turn into beautiful butterflies or moths when they grow up!

Length: 1 in

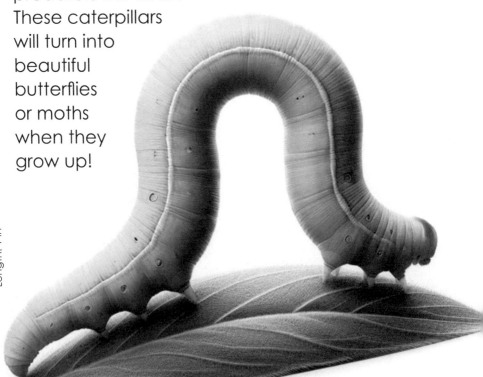

Jewel Beetle

Did you know they come in metallic colors?

Their shiny bodies come in stunning colors like metallic green, blue, and red, that sparkle in the sunlight, making them look like little jewels! These beetles are excellent flyers and can zoom around flowers and trees with ease.

Jewel beetles also have strong jaws that help them chew through wood, where they often lay their eggs.

Length: 2.55 in

KKatydid

Did you know they have ears on their front legs?

They use these ears to listen for sounds like other katydids singing or predators approaching. Speaking of singing, katydids are great singers! They produce sounds by rubbing their wings together, creating a song that can be heard at night in forests and gardens.

Katydid colors and patterns help them blend into leaves and branches, making them hard to spot. These insects are masters of disguise and music in the insect world!

Length: 2.4 in

Ladybug

Did you know they come in different colors?

They can be red, orange, yellow, and even black with spots, which help protect them from predators by warning that they might taste bad or be poisonous.

Ladybugs love to eat aphids, which are tiny insects that can harm plants. They're like tiny pest control superheroes for gardens!
Ladybugs can also fly, and they fold their delicate wings under their colorful shell when they're not flying.

Length: 0.3 in

Mosquito

Did you know only females bite?

They need blood to help them lay eggs. Male mosquitoes, on the other hand, feed on plant nectar. Mosquitoes can find their prey by sensing the carbon dioxide we breathe out and the heat of our bodies.

They have a sharp, straw-like mouthpart called a proboscis that they use to suck blood. Mosquitoes are not just pesky—they play a role in nature as food for other animals and help pollinate some plants.

Length: 0.3 in

Nymphalidae

Did you know they come in many beautiful colors and patterns?

Each species has its own unique design on its wings, like a work of art. These Nymphalidae butterflies are also great at migrating long distances. Some travel thousands of miles during their annual migrations!

Nymphalidae butterflies love to drink nectar from flowers using their long tongues, called proboscises. They play an important role in pollinating flowers and helping plants grow.

Length: 3.5 in

Orb weaver Spider

Did you know they spin really large webs?

These intricate, wheel-shaped webs are designed to catch flying insects like flies and mosquitoes. Orb-weaver spiders are skilled architects. They rebuild their webs every day to keep them strong and effective.

These spiders are not harmful to humans and play an important role in controlling insect populations. Some orb-weaver spiders are brightly colored or have interesting patterns on their bodies.

Length: 4.5 in

Praying Mantis

Did you know they can turn their heads 180°?

This helps them look behind them, to spot prey like flies and other insects. Praying mantises are excellent hunters. They have powerful front legs with spiky claws that they use to catch and hold their food.

These insects are also masters of camouflage, blending in with leaves and branches to hide from predators.

Length: 3.5 in

Queen Bee

Did you know they are the largest in the colony?

They have a special job to lay eggs to help the colony grow. A queen bee can lay up to 2,000 eggs in a single day! Queen bees are fed a special substance called royal jelly when they are larvae, which helps them develop into queens.

They live much longer than worker bees, often for several years, compared to just a few weeks for worker bees. Without a healthy queen bee, the colony cannot survive.

Length: 1 in

Rhinoceros Beetle

Did you know males have horns like a rhino?

These horns are used for fighting other males for territory and mates. Rhinoceros beetles are really strong. They can lift objects many times heavier than themselves using their powerful legs.

Despite their large size and horns, they're harmless to humans and mainly eat decaying wood and fruit.

S Stink bug

Did you know they release a smelly odor?

This stinky smell released when they feel threatened helps them fend off predators like birds and frogs. Stink bugs come in various colors, from brown to green to red, and they have shield-shaped bodies that protect their wings.

These insects are plant feeders, munching on crops like tomatoes and soybeans, which sometimes makes them pests for farmers. Stink bugs are also tough survivors. They can survive freezing temperatures by finding warm places to hide.

Length: 0.6 in

Termite

Did you know they live in large colonies?

Their colonies can include millions of termites. They work together to build elaborate nests made of chewed wood, saliva, and mud. Termites are tiny but powerful. They can eat through wood, causing damage to buildings and trees.

Despite their reputation as pests, termites are important for breaking down dead wood and recycling nutrients back into the soil. Some termites can even produce a loud noise by banging their heads against the walls of their nests to warn others of danger.

Length: 0.35 in

UUnderwing Moth

Did you know they have hidden hindwings?

When they're disturbed, they flash these colorful bright hindwings to surprise predators! Underwing moths are also great at camouflage. They blend in perfectly with tree bark or leaves during the day.

These moths are nocturnal, meaning they're active at night and rest during the day. Some underwing moth species have wingspans of over 3 inches, making them some of the larger moths you might see fluttering around at night.

Length: 2.75 in

Velvet ant

Did you know they are a type of wingless wasp?

They have a fuzzy appearance and come in vibrant colors like red, orange, and black. Velvet ants are known for their painful sting.

Some species have one of the most potent insect stings in the world! However, only female velvet ants can sting; males are harmless.

These ants are solitary and spend their time searching for the nests of other insects to lay their eggs.

Length: 0.75 in

W

Wasp

Did you know not all types of wasps sting?

Some wasps are important pollinators, just like bees!
Wasps have a narrow waist between their thorax and
abdomen, which gives them a distinctive shape.

They build nests out of paper-like material made from
chewed wood fibers mixed with saliva.
Wasps are also hunters. They catch
and eat other insects, which
helps control pest
populations in
gardens and
forests.

Length: 0.6 in

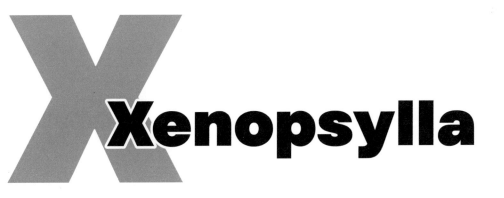

Xenopsylla

Did you know they are incredible jumpers?

Xenopsylla fleas can leap up to 150 times their body length, which is like a person jumping the length of a football field! Fleas have special mouthparts designed for piercing skin and sucking blood, which they need to survive.

These tiny insects are known for bothering pets and sometimes humans, but they play an important role in ecosystems by being the primary source of nutrition for other species.

Length: 0.125 in

Yellowjacket

Did you know they are a type of wasp?

They are known for their bright yellow and black stripes. Yellowjackets are social insects that live in large colonies with a queen and worker wasps.

Yellowjackets are carnivorous. They hunt insects and scavenge for food like meat and sugary substances. They can sting multiple times if they feel threatened, so it's important to be cautious around them.

Length: 0.5 in

Zebra jumping spider

Did you know they have black and white stripes?

These spiders are tiny but mighty. They can jump many times their body length to catch prey like flies and mosquitoes. Zebra Jumping Spiders have excellent vision and use it to hunt during the day.

They don't build webs to catch food but instead pounce on their prey with lightning-fast reflexes. These spiders are harmless to humans.

Length: 0.2 in

Made in the USA
Columbia, SC
24 September 2024

42600508R00015